I Like Big Mutts and I Cannot Lie!

Fun Facts About Man's Best Friend

By Erin Best

For Charlotte, my affectionate Jack Russell Terrier, and my supportive family.

"May I be what my dog thinks I am"

Our canine companions bring so much joy to our lives. They provide unconditional love, companionship, laughter...and the occasional mess. So what makes these loveable pooches the leading candidate for the position of Man's best friend? Here's what you should know about your wagging bundle of joy...

Dogs have developed more advanced social and communicative behaviour with humans than any other animal, including primates. Not only can dogs understand human social cues such as pointing, they will follow a human's gaze to locate objects.

Studies have even demonstrated dogs' unique ability to understand the perspective of humans. Dogs will often refrain from eating food without permission if it is located in front of a window, suggesting dogs understand that humans can see them being naughty through the window. In contrast, many dogs will indulge in forbidden food when there is no window allowing them to be caught. Similarly, dogs will choose to beg for food from a person whose vision has not been obstructed, suggesting they understand when humans can and cannot see them begging for food.

Research into the communicative behaviours between dogs and humans have shown that the facial recognition patterns of dogs match those of humans. When perceiving human faces, dogs demonstrate a left-gaze bias, meaning we have a preference for gazing to the left, or inspecting the right hand side of a face first and for longer periods. This is observed in both humans and dogs, however, dogs only demonstrate this when looking at human faces and not with other dogs or animals. This suggests a specific communicative behaviour developed for interacting with humans as part of the domestication process.

Studies have shown that yawning is contagious between humans and dogs! Contagious yawning has only been observed in humans, chimps, baboons and dogs. This adds to the overwhelming evidence that dogs have a special bond with humans and may suggest a specialized ability to empathize with their humans.

Do dogs feel guilty when they know they have been naughty? Possibly...though it is thought that dogs are so adept in reading human body language that they respond accordingly when they see our reaction to that chewed up slipper!

A secret technique for training many dogs (even the naughty ones) – warm barbeque chicken! Open a zip lock bag of skinless chicken pieces during a training session and you'll have the attention of every dog within smelling range.

For dogs who are watching their weight, or are not particularly motivated by food (in which case, you may have yourself a cat), plenty of positive reinforcement in the form of praise, their favourite toy, and pats will work equally well.

The shape and size of dog skulls vary greatly between breeds, and are classified according to the Cephalic, or Cranial, Index. *Dolichocephalic* dogs have long heads and muzzles, such as the handsome Afghan Hound and Greyhound. *Mesocephalic* dogs have medium sized, less elongated skulls and appear to have equally proportioned muzzles, such as the Labrador Retriever and Border Collie. *Brachycephalic* dogs have a broad, short skull and muzzle, and are renowned for snoring and respiratory problems, such as the Boxer and Pug.

Dogs' ears can give us a clue as to the specific purposes for which they were bred, or their special talents, if you will. Dogs with long, floppy ears are often scent dogs. Their floppy ears help to stir up and channel scent particles from the ground to the dog's snout. Dogs with pricked up ears are often sight dogs, and use their erect ears to accurately locate the source of sounds.

If you own a terrier breed, you have probably noticed your dog has a habit of vigorously shaking their toys from side to side. This instinctive behaviour is mostly observed in breeds that were used for ratting. The quick shaking motion swiftly kills rodents, and this action is instinctive when your dog is playing with their toys.

Dogs regulate their body temperature by panting, and sweating through the pads of their feet. Owners should ensure their dogs have access to plenty of fresh water as, like humans, dogs suffer from heat stroke. Never leave your dog unattended in a car – the temperature inside a car can more than double in a short amount of time. This can be fatal, as dogs cannot effectively regulate their body temperature in a hot car.

Newfoundlands are remarkable swimmers due to their webbed paws. By contrast, the stubby legs and long, heavy-set bodies of Basset Hounds make swimming a difficult task for this breed.

Studies suggest dogs not only have the ability to recognize familiar barks from other dogs, they can also interpret information from the type of bark. Perhaps not quite to the extent of the "Twighlight Bark" in 101 Dalmatians, but impressive nonetheless.

Wolves and wild dogs, such as dingoes, bark far less than domestic dogs. Contrary to popular belief, wild dogs do have the ability to bark, though domestic dogs are much more vocal in their communicative behaviours. It is thought that this is due to their interactions with humans.

Dingoes are thought to be descendants of domesticated dogs from East Asia, brought over to Australia on boats roughly 4,600

to 5,400 years ago. Scientific evidence suggests dingoes appear to be related to the Indian Wolf.

Unlike humans, dogs walk on their toes, allowing them to cover longer distances at a faster speed. As well as outperforming humans in sprinting and cross country, the powerful hind leg muscles of dogs make them outstanding athletes at high jump, with some breeds able to jump four times their own height.

Dogs do not have collar bones – their shoulders are held in place by a sling of muscles.

Dogs have a structure in their eyes that functions like an extra eyelid, called a nictitating membrane. Next time your dog is feeling a little drowsy you may notice a white membrane in the corner of their eye. This membrane helps to protect and lubricate the eye.

The Chinese breeds Chow Chow and Shar Pei are well known for their uniquely coloured blue/black tongue.

The stylish haircut of French Poodles was originally designed as a practical means of keeping these dogs warm when used as water retrievers. Poodles were shorn to help keep them afloat when swimming, leaving long hair only over vital areas of their body for protection. The tufts of hair remaining cover their head, chest, kidneys and ankles, which protects their organs and joints from the cold water.

Unlike most other breeds of dog that have double coats, poodles have only a single layer of dense fur with no undercoat, and are thought to be hypoallergenic. Contrary to popular belief, poodle fur does shed minimally, but tangles in the surrounding fur rather than falling off the dog. This means poodles require regular grooming to avoid matted fur and bad hair days.

Greyhounds can reach speeds of up to 70 kilometres per hour. Their impressive athleticism is owed to their large heart, high percentage of fast twitch muscle fibres, high levels of red blood cells and their "double suspension gallop", in which all four paws come off the ground when contracting and extending the legs.

As dogs run faster, their paws come closer together on impact with the ground. So next time you are tracking your run away pooch, you can determine their speed depending on whether there is four, two or one paw print left in the soil.

Dogs do not have thumbs – they have non-functional dewclaws located on the inside of their front legs. Some dogs also have rear dewclaws on their hind legs, often attached only by skin.

Contrary to popular belief, dogs are not completely colour blind. Dogs can see blue and yellow, however, they do have difficulty differentiating between red and green, much like red-green colour blindness in humans.

Dogs are much better at seeing movement than stationary objects. Their vision is thought to have evolved in such a way to assist in hunting. Next time your dog can't find his tennis ball sitting in the grass, try throwing it for him!

Dogs have better vision in low light than humans. This is due to their larger pupils allowing more light to enter the eye, an abundance of light sensitive cells called rods, and a mirror-like membrane at the back of the eye called a tapetum lucidum. This membrane rebounds light to the retina, allowing a greater amount of light to be absorbed and thus better vision in dark environments.

As many owners are aware, dogs have far superior hearing to humans. Your dog knows when your car is approaching from an impressive distance due to their ability to hear sounds up to four times further away than humans. In addition, dogs perceive a greater range of frequencies, hearing between 67-45,000 Hz, compared to the human range of approximately 64-23,000 Hz.

Foods such as chocolate, macadamia nuts, onion, grapes and raisins are toxic to dogs. These foods contain ingredients that can seriously damage your dog's health and can even be fatal. If your dog eats some of your Easter Eggs, contact your local veterinarian, who may need to induce vomiting. Instead of chocolate, try a pet friendly carob treat to spoil your dog.

There are 701 breeds of dogs worldwide. This genetic variability reflects our canine companions' status as man's best friend, and the result of hundreds of years of both natural and artificial selection.

The physical characteristics of dog breeds demonstrate selective breeding for specific purposes. Scent hounds (for example the Basset Hound) have long floppy ears, to assist their sensitive noses in tracking smells by keeping the scent in the air close to the dog's nose. In addition, their moist, droopy lips help to catch scent particles.

Sight hounds, such as the Whippet, were bred for speed and agility with their athletic bodies and superior vision.

Sporting dogs, such as the Labrador Retriever, were used to find and return game for hunters, and have soft mouths to help prevent damaging the game when carried in the dog's mouth. Some breeds even have water resistant coats and webbed feet for retrieving game from the water.

Terriers were bred to be compact and hardy for hunting small animals in confined spaces. As their name suggests, Fox Terriers were bred to continue the pursuit of the fox after the hounds had run him to ground. They are small enough to enter the den and traditionally had docked tails for the hunter to grasp and pull them back out of the hole. Jack Russell Terriers were bred from Fox Terriers for hunting rats and other vermin. The energetic and brave temperament of many terrier breeds is well suited for such jobs.

Working dogs are usually large and strong, such as the St Bernard, who was used as a search and rescue dog in the snow. According to legend, St Bernards wore a barrel containing brandy around their neck for avalanche victims to drink in order to keep warm until rescued.

Herding dogs, such as the Border Collie, have great stamina and a weatherproof double coat for protection from extreme weather conditions while herding livestock. These breeds will often have a very strong instinct to round up animals and even family members.

Toy breeds, such as the Maltese, were mainly used as status symbols and a source of warmth. Given that a dog's body temperature is higher than ours, it was handy to have lap dogs to keep owners' laps and beds warm inside chilly castles – a furry hot water bottle that never goes cold!

You may have noticed a variety of tail shapes between breeds. While tails generally assist in communication (who hasn't noticed how fast that tail wags when it's walk-o-clock, compared to tightly tucked under the tooshie at bath time), some breeds use their tails for additional purposes. Cold weather breeds such as the Husky, Alaskan Malamute and Spitz, have fluffy tails that curl forward. This helps keep their nose warm when they curl into a little ball to sleep. Breeds that enjoy the water, such as the Labrador Retriever, have otter-like tails that work like rudders for swimming.

Most dog owners are aware that dogs use visual cues such as tail wagging to communicate. Research suggests the direction in which a dog wags their tail provokes different responses from other dogs. When reading tail wagging signals in their canine pals, dogs tend to be more relaxed when the wags slightly more to the right. By contrast, if the tails wags slightly to the left, dogs appear to respond in a more stressful way. Another good reason to support anti-tail docking laws (tail docking is now banned in all states of Australia).

Dog's whiskers are specialised, sensitive hairs that are used as sensory receptors. There are networks of nerves located at the root of each whisker, allowing dogs to feel their way around in the dark, and even sense subtle changes such as vibrations. This is how your dog is able to predict thunderstorms before they arrive!

If you do not plan to become a breeder, having your dog speyed/neutered has many benefits. This procedure can significantly reduce the risk of cancer and other diseases of the reproductive organs, reduce the risk of mammary cancer and infections of the uterus in female dogs, improve undesirable behaviour, and increase their overall health and quality of life.

While humans rely mainly on their sight to navigate and interpret the world, dogs primarily use their sense of smell. The abundance of olfactory receptors in a dog's nose (anywhere between 125 million to 300 million scent glands, compared to approximately 5 million in humans) makes them expert sniffers, and much better at coping with reduced vision or hearing than humans. In addition, although the size of a dog's brain is significantly smaller than ours, the section of the brain responsible for smell is approximately 40 times larger in dogs than humans. This means your dog's sense of smell is approximately 1000 times better than yours.

Dogs have a wet nose to assist them in smelling. The thin mucous covering on your dog's nose helps them capture scent particles. They are also able to locate the direction of smells by moving their nostrils independently – a skill most humans are yet to perfect.

Some specially trained dogs are able to detect cancers with their trusty snouts. Dogs can smell chemicals associated with cancerous tissues, detected in breath, sweat and urine.

Police dogs are able to locate humans by detecting the scent of skin flakes, sweat and scent mists for up to 105 hours!

Bloodhounds have such a strong sense of smell that they are the only animal whose evidence is admissible in a court of law.

Dogs will sometimes sneeze out of excitement or nervousness, as the nerves in their nasal passages can be over-stimulated.

Dogs have the ability to sniff and breathe as two separate functions. While dogs breathe in the same way as humans, they also sniff short breaths of air to maintain remnants of a scent in the nasal canal that is not exhaled.

Puppies possess a specialised heat sensor located in their noses to assist them in locating their mother while their eyes and ears are closed. This special sixth sense begins to disappear as they get older and can use their other senses.

Dogs have an extra olfactory chamber in their noses called the vomeronasal organ, or Jacobson's organ, which contain of a pair of elongated sacs with olfactory receptors. These receptors are distinct from those in the nasal cavity.

Ever noticed your dog's ears are quite mobile and can move almost right to the back of their heads? More than a dozen muscles control their ear movements to assist in locating the source of sound.

Unlike humans, dogs' ear canals are L-shaped, descending straight down towards the jaw and turning horizontally towards the ear drum. This is why many dogs are prone to ear infections or foreign bodies when water or debris become trapped in the ear canal. If your dog has long, floppy ears, flipping the ears inside out to air off after a swim may help to dry out the ear canal.

Along with many other impressive senses that humans lack, dogs are sensitive to the Earth's magnetic field.

Specially trained seizure alert dogs are able to detect oncoming seizures in humans and alert their owners up to an hour before the onset.

Studies have shown that dog owners maintain better health and wellbeing than those who do not own a dog. Dog ownership has been linked to a reduction in minor physical ailments, as well as the prevention of serious medical conditions such as heart disease. In addition, studies have suggested dogs are great facilitators in the recovery from ill health...as any dog lover will tell you.

So there you have it. Dogs have been by our side for thousands of years, learning to communicate specifically with humans, assisting us with their specialised skills, and providing endless entertainment. Now that's what I call loyalty.

"He is your friend, your partner, your defender, your dog. You are his life, his love, his leader. He will be yours, faithful and true, to the last beat of his heart. You owe it to him to be worthy of such devotion"

Further reading:

Hare, B. & Tomasello, M. (2005). Human-like social skills in dogs? Trends in Cognitive Sciences, 9(9),

439-444.

Horowitz, A. (2009). Inside of a dog: What dogs see, smell and know. New York, NY: Scribner.

Wells, D. (2007). Domestic dogs and human health: An overview. British Journal of Health

Psychology, 12, 145-156.

Manufactured by Amazon.ca
Bolton, ON